END ADDICTION

A Revised Handbook To Help You Realise And Break That Habit.

By: Josh Akhtar

Table of Contents

Chapter One: Drug Misuse, Abuse, And Addiction: What's The Difference?

Addiction is an inability to quit taking a drug or participating in a habit even while it is inflicting psychological and bodily damage.

The word addiction does not simply relate to dependency on narcotics such as heroin or cocaine. Some addictions may entail an inability to cease indulging in activities such as gambling, eating, or working.

Addiction is a persistent illness that may also occur from using drugs. In reality, the overuse of opioids — notably illicitly produced fentanyl — caused approximately 50,000 death Trusted Source in the United States in 2019 alone.

The American Society of Addiction Medicine describes addiction as "a curable, chronic medical condition involving intricate interactions among brain circuits, heredity, the environment, and an individual's life experiences. People with addiction use drugs or participate in activities that become obsessive and typically persist despite detrimental consequences."

Many individuals, although not all, start taking a substance or initially participate in an activity deliberately. However, addiction may take over and impair self-control.

Addiction is a significant, persistent dependency on a drug or activity. The prevalence of addiction costs the U.S. economy hundreds of billions of dollars per year.

A person with addiction is unable to quit taking a drug or participating in an activity even when it has adverse impacts on everyday functioning.

Addiction vs. Misuse

Drug addiction and drug abuse are distinct.

Overuse refers to the misuse of a drug at excessive dosages or in improper conditions that might lead to health and social consequences.

However, not everyone who misuses a drug develops an addiction. Addiction is the fact or state of being addicted to a certain drug, item, or activity.

For example, a person who drinks alcohol extensively on a night out may feel both the pleasurable and dangerous effects of the chemical.

However, this does not qualify as an addiction unless the individual suffers a chronic, relapsing condition marked by obsessive drug seeking, sustained use despite detrimental consequences, and long-lasting alterations in the brain.

There is drug addiction and non-substance addiction. Some instances of non-substance addiction include:

- Gambling
- Food
- Internet
- Gaming
- Cell phone
- Sex etc

Someone with an addiction will continue to abuse the drug or activity despite the detrimental consequences it produces.

Drug usage, misuse, and addiction are all severe public health concerns. Since all of these relationships with the use of illicit drugs and incorrect use of legal substances (e.g., cigarettes, alcohol, prescription medicine), a lot of people routinely use these words interchangeably. However, the interventions for each condition substantially differ. That's why accurately recognizing a person's drug issue is vital. Read on to grasp the essential distinctions between drug misuse, abuse, and addiction.

What is Drug Misuse?

Drug usage is usually related to prescribed drugs. Prescription drugs are designed to be taken as advised by physicians. This is because these sorts of medicines might have harmful side effects if guidelines are not followed.

Drug abuse arises when these drugs are consumed for a purpose that is not compatible with legal or medical criteria. Examples of this include:

- Taking the improper dosage
- Taking the medication at the wrong moment
- Forgetting to take a dosage
- Stopping the usage of medicine too soon
- Taking medicine for purposes other than those they were given
- Taking a medicine that was not prescribed to you

What is Drug Abuse?

Drug abuse arises when drugs, including alcohol, illegal narcotics, or other psychoactive chemicals, are overused to get high or inflict self-harm. It is also known as Substance Use Disorder (SUD) as persons who take substances suffer profoundly changed thinking, behavior, and physiological functioning.

What is Drug Addiction?

Drug addiction, often known as severe Drug Use Illness (SUD), is a brain disorder that emerges as the uncontrolled use of a substance notwithstanding its consequences. People with drug addiction have a physical and/or psychological urge to use a substance because they experience significant or devastating withdrawal symptoms when they go without that substance.

How is Drug Misuse Different From Drug Abuse?

The major distinction between a person who misuses drugs and a person who abuses drugs is their purpose. The former takes medicine to address a particular condition, while the latter uses a substance to evoke certain sensations.

An example of drug abuse is when a person who can't fall asleep after taking a single sleeping medication takes another tablet an hour later expecting that "it'll do the job." However, it's drug misuse when a person uses sleeping drugs to control their emotions or get a "buzz," or — in worst-case circumstances — to commit suicide.

How is Drug Abuse Different From Drug Addiction?

Drug addiction is a severe type of drug misuse. The contrast between the two illnesses resides in how much control the person can exercise over oneself. Since a person who takes drugs still maintains control over their life, they don't face severe disturbance in their life.

In contrast, persons with an addiction have a problem that impacts most if not all parts of their life. They frequently miss jobs or school, harm their family physically and/or financially, experience health difficulties, get into legal difficulties, and have other major concerns due to their drug use. But despite this, they are unable to modify their routines to better their circumstances. This is why many individuals with drug addiction become unemployed, homeless, or estranged from their families. Some even die from their drug usage.

How can you receive assistance for drug misuse, abuse, and addiction?

Since drug usage isn't a sickness, a simple scolding may help solve the situation. However, recurrent drug misuse may readily lead to drug abuse and ultimately addiction. This is because it may lead to increased drug tolerance and then drug reliance when cognitive, behavioral, and physiological difficulties occur.

In drug addiction instances, honest dialogue regarding drug usage and its effects might drive a person to change as they still have a choice over their conduct. It's crucial nevertheless that they grasp all the psychological, social, legal, emotional, and spiritual implications of drug misuse.

On the other hand, willpower is not enough to modify the behavior of a person with drug addiction. As their bodies are already biologically reliant on a drug, they would require medication. The treatment normally begins with a medically supervised detoxification phase to manage the symptoms of drug withdrawal.

A mental health expert then works with the patient to build a rehabilitation plan toward sobriety. This plan may incorporate frequent attendance at support group meetings and follow-up treatment sessions to ensure that the patient has the skills and methods to assist them to maintain a happy and healthy lifestyle.

Chapter Two: What Are The Symptoms Of Addiction?

Symptoms of Addiction

The major indicators of addiction are:

- Declining grades or trouble at school
- Poor performance at work
- Relationship issues, which sometimes entail lashing out against others who detect the addiction
- An unwillingness to quit taking a drug even if it may be creating health concerns or other problems, such as troubles with job or relationships
- An obvious loss of energy in regular tasks
- Profound changes in appearance, including weight loss and a visible disregard for cleanliness

- Appearing defensive when questioned about drug usage

Addiction is a disorder with a spectrum of hazardous circumstances and behaviors. Recognizing these indications may help a person with addiction obtain the therapy they need.

Doctors now classify addictions under a category called “substance-related and addictive disorders.”

The key symptom of an addiction is a problematic pattern of use, which leads to clinically substantial impairment or suffering.

The particular symptoms differ according to the addiction condition.

A person with a drug use problem finds it difficult to manage their usage of a certain substance. They continue taking a drug or participating in addictive behavior, even though they may be aware of the damage it might bring or when obvious proof of harm is visible.

Powerful desires also define addiction. The person may not be able to cease partaking in the addictive drug or activity despite expressing a wish to quit.

The indications and symptoms of drug use disorder might vary with the individual, the substance or activity they are overusing, their family history, and their particular circumstances.

The signs of addiction can lead to a 'domino effect' of unpleasant conditions.
Substance use disorders entail a spectrum of psychological, physical, and social repercussions that may dramatically diminish people's quality of life.

Symptoms of Addiction may be largely separated into three primary categories, as below:

1. Psychological symptoms
2. Social symptoms
3. Physical symptoms

While we will break the symptoms into these three groups, the truth is less apparent. Many of these symptoms overlap and may lead to one another.

An example of this overlap is when someone has the psychological consequence of desiring to divert money from their usual food store to acquiring a drug, and then not ingesting enough nutrition.

Likewise, marital troubles and a developing aversion to social engagements may lead to and aggravate psychological disorders, including sadness and anxiety.

Psychological Symptoms

Symptoms of addiction that induce mental illnesses include the following.

An inability to quit using: In many circumstances, such as a dependency on nicotine, alcohol, or other drugs, a person will have made at least one serious but failed effort to give up. This could also be physiological, since certain narcotics, such as heroin, are chemically addictive and create withdrawal symptoms if a person stops using them.

Use and misuse of drugs persist despite health problems: The person keeps frequently using the drug, even when they have acquired linked ailments. For example, a smoker may continue smoking after the development of a lung or heart condition. They may or may not be aware of the health consequences of the drug or activity.

Dealing with difficulties: A person with addiction usually feels the need to consume the substance or carry out the activity to cope with their troubles.

Obsession: A person may get obsessed with a drug, spending more and more time and energy discovering methods of acquiring their substance, and in certain circumstances how they may use it.

Taking risks: An person with an addiction may take risks to get the substance or participate in the habit, such as exchanging sex or stealing for illegal drugs, drug money, or the drugs themselves. While under the influence of certain drugs, a person with substance use disorder may engage in unsafe actions, such as rapid and dangerous driving or violence.

Taking an initial big dose: This is frequent with alcohol use disorder. The person may fast drink big amounts of alcohol to experience the effects and feel good.

Social Symptoms

Using drugs may lead to loneliness and secrecy: Substance use disorder can alter the way a person socializes with and connects to other people.

Sacrifices: A person with drug abuse could give up certain activities that formerly provided them delight. For example, a person with alcohol consumption disorder may reject an offer to go camping or spend a day on a boat if no alcohol is available. A person with a nicotine habit may opt not to meet up with pals if they intend to go to a smoke-free bar or restaurant.

Dropping hobbies and activities: As an addiction advances, the person may cease indulging in pursuits they like. People who are addicted to cigarettes, for example, could discover they can no longer physically deal with taking part in their preferred sport.

Maintaining a good supply: People with drug use disorders will constantly make sure they have a good supply, even if they do not have much money. They may make concessions in their household budget to assure the availability of the drug.

Secrecy and solitude: In many circumstances, a person with a drug use problem may use the substance alone or in secret.

Denial: A considerable proportion of persons with drug use disorder are not aware that they have a problem. They could be aware of physical dependency on a drug but reject or refuse to recognize the need to seek treatment, thinking that they can stop "anytime" they want to.

Excess consumption or abuse of substances: Some forms of drug use disorders, such as alcohol or opiate use disorders, may cause a person to consume dangerous quantities of a substance. The physical ramifications of misusing a drug may be severe and include overdose. However, for a person with a drug use disorder, these effects will not be adequate to prevent future misuse.

Having stashes: A person with an addiction may keep tiny stockpiles of a drug stashed away in various sections of the home or automobile, frequently in unusual locations, to prevent discovery.

Legal issues: This is more a hallmark of certain alcohol and illegal substance dependences. Legal difficulties may emerge either because the drug affects judgment or drives the person to take additional risks to the level of creating public disruption or violence or breaching the law to receive the substance in the first place.

Financial difficulties: An costly drug might lead to large and recurring financial sacrifices to get a regular supply.

Physical Symptoms

The distribution technique of a chemical might cause harm. Smoking a drug, for example, may harm the lungs. Repeatedly using a drug may influence several body processes and systems.

Withdrawal symptoms: When levels of the drug to which a person has dependent drop below a specific level, they could suffer physical symptoms, depending on the substance. These include cravings, constipation, diarrhea, shaking, convulsions, sweating, and atypical behavior, including aggression.

Appetite changes: Some drugs modify a person's appetite. Marijuana intake, for example, can considerably boost their appetite while cocaine may lessen it.

Damage or sickness from using a substance: Smoking substances, for example, tobacco and crack, may lead to irreversible respiratory disorders and lung malignancies. Injecting illegal narcotics may lead to limb injury and difficulties with veins and arteries, in some circumstances leading to the development of infection and probable loss of a limb. Regularly ingesting an excessive quantity of alcohol might lead to chronic liver disorders.

Sleeplessness: Insomnia is a frequent symptom of withdrawal. Using illegal stimulants, such as speed or ecstasy, could also induce a disturbed sleep pattern since a person might stay up late for many nights in a row to go to parties and take the drug.

A change in appearance: A person may begin to seem more disheveled, fatigued, and haggard, as consuming the drug or carrying out the addicted activity replaces crucial sections of the day, like cleaning clothing and attending to personal hygiene.

Increasing tolerance: The body experiences decreasing effects of the drug with time, so a person feels the need to take more to have the same impact.
A person could suffer a few of these symptoms or many of them. Substance use disorder may have a significantly varied influence on every person.

Substance use disorder includes several symptoms that may cause harm to an individual's bodily and psychological health, daily activities, and social life.

The consequences vary largely on the sort of drug, personal circumstances, family life, a person's degree of knowledge about their conduct, and their present income.

Psychologically, a drug use disorder may lead to persistent usage despite negative repercussions on health and an inability to cease using. A person could be obsessed with obtaining hold of a drug or indulging in detrimental actions.

Substance and addictive behaviors could also lead to a retreat from personal duties, formerly essential activities, and social connections. They may cause a person to seek seclusion and participate in the drug use disorder in secret.

Substance use disorder may also lead to conflicts with the law, both in getting a substance and carrying out unusual or disorderly activities that stem from the use of the substance.

Regularly consuming a substance might potentially cause bodily harm, depending on the sort of drug. Some drugs generate withdrawal symptoms that involve several bodily consequences, such as shaking, sweating, or nausea.

If a person or someone they know has any of these symptoms, they should seek treatment for themselves or the person they are worried about, as soon as possible.

The initial indicators of addiction primarily rely on the drug used. Generally, the individual should pay attention to the amount of the drug they are consuming. Using the drug in bigger and larger doses should be a warning signal to the individual that they may be on the way to addiction.

Chapter Three: Withdrawal From Substance Addiction

When a person has an addiction and ceases using the drug or participating in the activity, they may suffer various symptoms.

For people who have grown physically dependent on a drug, rapid withdrawal may induce numerous unpleasant symptoms, and, in extreme situations, it may be deadly.

What Is Withdrawal?

Withdrawal is the mix of physical and mental consequences a person feels when they quit using or decrease their intake of a substance such as alcohol and prescription or recreational medications.

If you have been taking a drug with a high potential for dependence and you quit suddenly or abruptly or you cut down your usage dramatically, you might suffer a range of withdrawal symptoms. The strength and length of these withdrawal symptoms might vary greatly, depending on the kind of substance and your biological make-up.

Withdrawal may be painful and perhaps hazardous in certain situations. For this reason, you should always speak to your doctor before discontinuing or lowering your drug usage.

Symptoms of Withdrawal

What does it feel like to go through withdrawal? Withdrawal symptoms differ based on the sort of substance you were using. Some symptoms typically connected with withdrawal include:

Changes in Appetite

Changes in Mood
Chills or Shivering
Congestion
Depression
Fatigue
Irritability
Muscle pain
Nausea
Restlessness
Runny nose
Shakiness
Sleeping troubles
Sweating
Tremors
Vomiting

In certain situations, more severe symptoms such as hallucinations, seizures, and delirium may also occur. The kind of substance you were taking, the period you were taking it, and the dose you were taking may all impact the type and intensity of the symptoms you experience.

While the physical symptoms of withdrawal could last just a few days or a week, the psychological withdrawal, such as despair or dysphoria, might continue much longer.

Identifying Withdrawal

People may notice signs of withdrawal when they stop consuming or cut down on a drug. Missing your customary morning cup of coffee, for example, can result in symptoms of caffeine withdrawal such as weariness, headache, and irritability.

Symptoms of withdrawal are a symptom of reliance on a drug. You should speak to your doctor before you decrease or stop taking a prescription or substance for guidance on how to do so safely and avoid any withdrawal symptoms. Your doctor may be able to assist if you are having problems controlling your symptoms and offer medical monitoring to guarantee your safety while you detox from a drug.

Your doctor will also be able to evaluate whether the symptoms you are experiencing are due to withdrawal or if they are the consequence of another ailment.

Causes of Withdrawal

The body and brain strive to maintain a state of equilibrium known as homeostasis. Taking a drug upsets that equilibrium, therefore your body needs to take efforts to compensate including adjusting the amounts of particular neurotransmitters. These drugs work on your brain's reward system, causing the release of neurotransmitters.

When you frequently consume a drug over a length of time, your body may acquire a tolerance and dependency on that chemical. Tolerance implies that it takes bigger dosages of the drug to produce the same effects that you first experienced, while dependence means that your body needs the substance to avoid suffering withdrawal symptoms.

If you quickly cease or reduce your consumption of the drug, your body is once again thrown off balance and symptoms of withdrawal may ensue. Such symptoms are typically both physical and mental and might be harmful depending on the kind of substance.

Withdrawal symptoms are generally the reverse of the effects of the drug. For example, alcohol is a depressive, so if you abruptly quit using alcohol, you can feel symptoms of overstimulation such as anxiety or restlessness.

Types of Withdrawal

The particular withdrawal symptoms you experience vary on the sort of substance you were using. Several different drug kinds might result in withdrawal, including the following:

Antidepressants
Barbiturates
Cannabis
Depressants
Hallucinogens
Inhalants
Opioids
Stimulants

The following are some instances of certain chemicals that may lead to withdrawal and the predicted duration of such symptoms:

Alcohol: Not everyone who quits drinking alcohol experiences withdrawal symptoms, but most individuals who quit abruptly after consuming enough alcohol for any period might have a broad variety of symptoms. Many times such symptoms will provoke a relapse.

Heroin: Those who have grown addicted to heroin endure some especially acute withdrawal symptoms, although even the worst of those symptoms will fade in five to seven days. However, for others, Post-Acute Withdrawal Syndrome (PAWS) might linger for weeks or even months.

Marijuana: Compared to alcohol and other substances, the withdrawal symptoms that marijuana users experience when they attempt to stop being on the low side. But, some of those effects are painful enough for individuals that they opt to go back to utilizing the substance.

Nicotine: Not everyone gets all of the same symptoms of nicotine withdrawal. As many who smoke know, a symptom of nicotine withdrawal may make it tough to quit cigarettes. There are things you may do to decrease such symptoms, too.

OxyContin (oxycodone): The severity of OxyContin and other prescription opioid withdrawal symptoms is largely connected to how long you have taken the medicine and how much you consumed. If you take the painkiller just as advised, you may not have any withdrawal symptoms at all or extremely minor ones.

Treatment of Withdrawal

Treatment for withdrawal involves support, care, and drugs that may reduce symptoms and avoid dangerous problems.

With certain drugs, individuals can cease their usage quickly and manage their withdrawal symptoms on their own. For example, a person may be able to stop coffee without help and manage the unpleasant effects on their own until they pass.

But quickly stopping drugs such as benzodiazepines or alcohol might be potentially harmful, so always see your doctor come up with a detox plan. Medically-assisted withdrawal may guarantee that you are safe and aid to lessen unpleasant withdrawal symptoms.

Withdrawal Medications

The drugs your doctor may prescribe to assist ease symptoms of withdrawal may differ based on the sort of substance you were consuming.
These drugs may also be used to address certain withdrawal symptoms. These may include anti-anxiety meds, anticonvulsants, antipsychotics, or other treatments meant to alleviate nausea or sleep issues.

According to the National Institute on Drug Abuse, in most situations, the symptoms associated with drug withdrawal are readily addressed with drugs that minimize or eliminate the pain. But, treating withdrawal is not the same as treating dependency or addiction itself.

Coping With Withdrawal

In addition to obtaining medical treatment, there are some things that you may do that may help you feel better while you go through the withdrawal process:

Ask for aid. Whether you are treating withdrawal on your own or under the guidance of a doctor, it is crucial to have social support. Tell a trustworthy friend or family member so that they may check in and encourage you along the procedure.

Eat well. Focus on eating healthful, well-balanced meals. Eating fried, greasy, or sugary meals may make you feel worse.

Exercise. Try to get some physical exercise each day. Stretching, walking, swimming, or other activities may help enhance your mood.

Drink lots of water. It is crucial to keep hydrated when you are going through withdrawal, particularly if you are suffering flu-like symptoms like nausea and vomiting.

Relieve symptoms using Over Counter (OTC) drugs. Use suitable OTC drugs at the suggested amounts if you are suffering symptoms such as headache, upset stomach, or diarrhea.

Sleep. While withdrawal may occasionally lead to sleeping issues, try to obtain a decent amount of rest. Work to develop a regular sleep pattern and practice appropriate sleep habits.

Stress management techniques like yoga and meditation may also help you deal with your withdrawal experience. Be careful to contact your doctor, though, if you are struggling to manage or if you notice any troubling symptoms.

Supporting a Loved One During Withdrawal

It might be stressful for both of you when your loved one is going through withdrawal. Withdrawal may be physically and emotionally draining, and your loved one will need all the help they can get.

Explore Treatment Options

One of the nicest things you can do is investigate therapy alternatives together. This way, you may better grasp what withdrawal involves and the best course of action. Withdrawal may be different for everyone, so choosing a treatment plan that will work for your loved one is vital. Your loved one may require support throughout withdrawal, which may entail outpatient, residential, or inpatient programs.

Care for Yourself

When caring for someone else, it is crucial to ensure that you also care for yourself. This may be stressful and demanding, so be sure to take care of yourself physically and mentally. This might mean taking time for yourself, ensuring you are attending to your needs, and checking in with yourself regularly. This way, you will be in the greatest possible position to help your loved one.

Be There for Them

One of the most crucial things you can do is just be there for your loved one at this tough time. Just by being there and accessible, you may give them amazing support. This might entail listening to them, offering a shoulder to weep on, and giving a reassuring presence. Sometimes, simply having someone there who cares may make all the difference.

Offer Practical Help

Withdrawal may typically accompany bodily symptoms including nausea, vomiting, and diarrhea. Your loved one could require assistance with basic chores like making meals, going to the toilet, and moving about. If feasible, offer to assist with these duties so your loved one may concentrate on recuperating.

When to Seek Medical Help

Severe and even life-threatening symptoms may occasionally follow withdrawal. If your loved one is suffering any of these symptoms, it's crucial to get medical care immediately:

Delusions
Difficulty breathing
Hallucinations
Loss of consciousness
Rapid heartbeat
Tremors or seizures

If you are ever unclear if your loved one requires medical assistance, err on the side of caution and get aid.

Chapter Four: When To Contact A Doctor

Anyone taking drugs, even socially, should discuss them with a doctor to ensure safe usage and monitor for signs or symptoms of addiction.

However, a person with addiction may not be ready or prepared to seek professional medical care, despite the severe consequences it is having on their health and welfare.

If a person has a drug overdose, everyone around them should seek emergency medical aid immediately. A person who has recovered from an overdose may desire to seek professional treatment to address their addiction.

When a person is ready and wants assistance with their addiction, they may decide to contact a medical expert to explore possibilities for treatment. These choices include rehab, counseling, detox, and medication.

When to Discuss Substance Use

If you suspect you have a problem with addictive drugs, bring it up with your doctor. Some indicators might indicate that you:

- Keep taking drugs or alcohol even if doing so creates issues
- Need to use more and more of these to stay feeling good
- Are you no longer interested in items you used to appreciate
- Aren't taking care of yourself or your hygiene
- Make an appointment for a checkup with your usual doctor. Primary care physicians deal with these difficulties regularly.

What to Expect

Your doctor is supposed to keep everything you tell them secret. They aren't authorized to report you to the police if you're taking illicit substances. If you're a minor and don't want your parents to find out what you discuss with your doctor, ask if they would keep it secret.

They will question what drugs you are taking, how much of them you use, and how frequently you use them. Your doctor will chat with you about what issues your drug or alcohol usage has caused you.

You'll also speak about any health disorders that might be connected to your drug use, such as depression or other mental health difficulties.

Chapter Five: Treatments

Medicinal discoveries and improvements in diagnostics have enabled the medical community to create several approaches to treating and overcoming addiction

Some approaches include:

- Medication-based therapy
- Behavioral treatment and counseling
- Medical gadgets to treat withdrawal
- Treating linked psychological issues, such as depression
- Ongoing care to limit the likelihood of recurrence

Addiction therapy is extremely customized and typically involves the assistance of the individual's community or family.

Treatment might take a long time and may be difficult. Addiction is a chronic illness with a variety of psychological and physical repercussions. Each drug or habit may necessitate distinct management strategies.

Addiction therapy might be tough, but it is frequently beneficial. The optimal kind of therapy relies on the drug and the presentation of the addiction, which differs from person to person. However, therapy generally requires medication, counseling, and community support.

The greatest strategy to assist a relative is to create trust so that they will feel that you have their best interests in mind.

Make sure that any dialogue regarding your worries does not occur while they are under the influence. Avoid condemning or humiliating them for their addictive actions. Instead, say something like, “I care about you and am concerned about your safety and health," and express your thoughts about their actions.

Remember, many individuals deny that they have had difficulties for a long period. If that occurs, do not confront them. Just tell them that you care and seek permission to keep checking in with them.

With numerous alternatives accessible, you may pick an addiction treatment plan that best meets your specific requirements.

Addiction therapy is not one-size-fits-all. Treatments may vary dependent on your requirements. You may select the therapy that works best for you depending on the drug you're abusing, the degree of care you require, your specific mental health needs, or what health care alternatives you can afford. Here are some of the most prevalent addiction therapies that have placed people on a successful road to recovery.

Detoxification

Medically-assisted detox helps you to clear your body of addictive chemicals in a safe atmosphere. This is useful since occasionally drug withdrawal may create unpleasant or even life-threatening bodily symptoms. Because detox does not cure the underlying behavioral reasons of the addiction, it is often used in tandem with other therapy.

Cognitive Behavioral Therapy

According to American Addiction Centers, Cognitive Behavioral Therapy (CBT) is a helpful treatment method since it can be utilized for many various forms of addiction including, but not limited to, food addiction, alcohol addiction, and prescription medication addiction. Not only may CBT help you understand your problematic behavioral patterns, but it can also help you learn to identify triggers and create coping techniques. CBT may be coupled with other treatment modalities as well.

Rational Emotive Behavior Therapy

Rational Emotive Behavior Therapy (REBT) might help you understand your negative ideas and teach you techniques to battle emotions of self-defeat. The purpose of REBT is to help you recognize that the power of rational thinking resides within yourself and is not tied to external conditions or pressures.

Contingency Management

Contingency Management (CM) may be used to treat a broad range of addictions including alcohol, drugs, and tobacco. Contingency management treatment supports your good conduct (eg keeping sober) by offering you real incentives. This form of therapy has been used effectively to fight recurrence, according to the National Institute on Drug Abuse.

12-Step Facilitation

Twelve-step facilitation treatment ("12-step programs") may be used to treat alcohol and drug dependence. It is a sort of group treatment that incorporates acknowledgment that addiction has numerous negative repercussions that might be social, emotional, spiritual, and physical. This style of treatment starts with acceptance, then continues to surrender to a higher power, then finally transfers to engagement in frequent group sessions. Programs like the popular Alcoholics Anonymous employ group meetings for discussion and mutual support.

Treatment with Medication

Medication may play an essential role in rehabilitation when paired with behavioral therapy. Certain drugs may be used to lower cravings, boost mood, and minimize addictive behaviors. For example, the FDA recently authorized lofexidine to assist lessen cravings and withdrawal symptoms in individuals getting treatment for opioid addiction. Medications like acamprosate may help lessen drinking habits.

If you or a loved one are battling an addiction, you don't need to fight the battle alone. Talk to a medical professional. There are proven therapies available that may help you overcome your addiction.

www.ingramcontent.com/pod-product-compliance
Lightning Source LLC
LaVergne TN
LVHW050348160826
845677LV00014B/3862
9798352188118